excellent as you are

excellent as you are

*A Woman's Book of
Confidence,
Comfort, and Strength*

Sue Patton Thoele

Conari Press

First published in 2009 by Conari Press,
an imprint of Red Wheel/Weiser, LLC
With offices at:
500 Third Street, Suite 230
San Francisco, CA 94107
www.redwheelweiser.com

Library of Congress Cataloging-in-Publication Data
Thoele, Sue Patton.
  Excellent as you are : a woman's book of confidence, comfort, and strength/ Sue Patton Thoele.
     p. cm.
  "Much of this material originally appeared in The woman's book of confidence"—T.p. verso.
  ISBN 978-1-57324-456-5 (alk. paper)
  1. Women—Conduct of life. 2. Self-confidence. I. Thoele, Sue Patton.
Woman's book of confidence. II. Title.
  BJ1610.T44 2009
  155.3'33—dc22

Cover and text design by Donna Linden
Typeset in Perpetua and Handsome
Cover photograph © John Foxx Images
Interior photographs are © John Foxx Images unless otherwise noted. Pages 23, 24, and 26 © Corbis. Pages 62 71, 80, and 83 © ImageState. Interior illustrations © ZiMa/iStockphoto.

Printed in Hong Kong
GWP
10 9 8 7 6 5 4 3 2 1

With loving kindness

and deep respect

may we honor our own

and others' excellence.

Table of Contents

Introduction:
Owning Your Own Excellence

Is believing we are excellent, just the way we are, always easy? Not for me. Like most psychotherapists and writers, I teach and write about issues with which I have grappled in the past or am wrestling with in the moment.

In 1990, when I began writing *The Woman's Book of Confidence: Meditations for Strength and Inspiration,* from which *Excellent As You Are* is taken, I was in the midst of a personal crisis of confidence that was liberally laced with grief. That year, my husband and I moved to Colorado from California, where I had a circle of treasured friends, a successful counseling career, two published books, and an exciting avocation acting with a local community theater group. Our nest was newly emptied, and I was flying high.

Crash! At best, I am a reluctant mover, but this move made me feel as if I were a potted houseplant that had been jerked from its cozy planter and flung unceremoniously onto a desert freeway. Pretty melodramatic, right? Well, those were the days when my Drama Queen persona was very active, and she felt bereft, angry at my husband who wanted the move, and certainly not excellent in any way. Luckily, writing is therapeutic *and* transportable (once the computer was operational and a computer genie found the book files that had somehow strayed into cyberspace).

The writing process slowly worked its magic, and I was increasingly able to practice what I teach. Tears flowed less regularly, nightmares lessened, and depression began to lift. Eventually, I could comfort myself when grief surfaced and acknowledge at least the *possibility* of my own excellence. As these changes took root, it became possible to look outside my Drama Queen interpretation of the move and tentatively begin a new Colorado life.

Ironically, acknowledging and accepting our own excellence—as imperfect as it may be at any given moment—helps give us the strength and confidence needed to continually evolve into our most authentic selves. It is much easier to understand and act upon what may be limiting our happiness and peace of mind when we explore our inner workings with attitudes of self-acceptance.

Mastering the art of owning our own excellence and supporting ourselves emotionally through self-acceptance and encouragement can lead to a deep inner friendship which, in turn, creates a sense of security and builds confidence. Such a friendship can be likened to a greenhouse in which delicate seedlings are given the best environment possible to foster growth. In the tender and gentle atmosphere of a nurturing greenhouse, plants and flowers (even when repotted) mature into their natural beauty. So, too, can the very essence of the self flourish.

If the emotional greenhouse you have been providing for yourself is drafty—if it doesn't sustain you in difficult times and enhance your life in good ones—you can rebuild it. We can learn to give ourselves a comforting climate of genuine self-love and respect, one that inspires us to bloom into our vast potential for wisdom, beauty, and service.

It is my wish and prayer that *Excellent As You Are* becomes a gentle greenhouse for you, a quiet place in which you can compassionately befriend and trust yourself. I hope the meditations and ideas in these pages act as small buds of encouragement, bringing you confidence in yourself just as you are now, not as you wish you were or think you *should* be. And may the breathtaking beauty of the photographs within help you recognize and celebrate your own beauty. From hearts overflowing with self-love and acceptance, we can more readily comfort, support, and inspire others. Let there be peace on Mother Earth, and let it begin in our own hearts and toward our own selves.

Sharing Roots

On a trip up the coast of California and Oregon, I learned a valuable lesson about mutual support from the majestic redwood trees that thrive there. Redwoods are inclusive beings—as they grow, they incorporate objects around them, including rocks and other trees, into their basic structure. Although redwoods have shallow roots, they are noted for their strength and longevity because they share their roots with others. Each individual tree is invited into the whole and, in turn, helps support the entire group. This adaptation appears to have worked brilliantly, for redwoods are among the oldest living things on earth.

Feminine energy is naturally inclusive. In order to survive and thrive, we need to learn to consciously share our roots with others, to ask for encouragement and support when we need it, and stand ready to give the same to those who come to us.

By sharing our roots of compassion and support, we women, like the redwoods, create a safety net in which the whole is greater than the sum of its parts.

I have the courage to ask for support when I need it.
I am willing to support others when they need my help.

Heeding Physical Clues

We can have confidence that our bodies have been given to us as miraculous vehicles for our consciousness, and it is our sacred duty to appreciate and care for them. No one but ourselves is privileged to the information our bodies give us. Only we can weave safety nets of personal health and well-being by heeding the clues of our wise and deserving bodies.

Sit quietly with your eyes closed and thank your body for its wisdom and the faithful way it serves you. Gently bless your body. With as much acceptance as you can, focus your attention on any pain or illness you are experiencing and ask your body what you need to do to help alleviate the discomfort. Open your heart and mind to recognizing and acting on the clues your body is giving you.

I encourage my body by listening to its wisdom.
I honor and care for my wondrous body by recognizing the clues it gives me.
I have the courage to explore the psychological causes of my illnesses.

Gathering Ourselves Together

Our lives are often like fall storms, flinging the leaves of our concentration and contentment to the four winds and causing us to wonder how we can keep on keeping on. When we feel fragmented, we are actually beside ourselves energetically and need to gather ourselves back together again.

Close your eyes and visualize your physical, emotional, and mental selves. After you see or sense these three aspects of yourself, envision your Higher Self—your spiritual part—above the other three. Softly say, "Together, together, together," three times—a total of nine togethers. As you repeat the words, picture the symbols for your physical, emotional, and mental aspects gathering together under, and finally into, your spiritual part. As you visualize, gently repeat the series of nine togethers until calm replaces chaos.

Even though this exercise may seem simplistic, it speaks powerfully to our subconscious minds and allows us to gather our energy together, thereby naturally balancing and harmonizing our feelings. Standing in our own skins, rather than being "beside ourselves," allows us to move constructively through our busy lives, feeling in sync.

I have the power to replace chaos with calm.
I balance and harmonize the four aspects of my being.

Finding a Hand Up
When We Bottom Out

There are times in each of our lives when it feels as though the pins have been kicked out from under us and we're absolutely sure we've bottomed out. Some of us feel guilty if we can't go it alone during such difficult times. But it's often healthier for us to ask for a hand up when we find ourselves in the pits. Trying to deal with things by ourselves can magnify our pain and lead to feelings of depression and isolation.

If you are grieving or in pain, ask yourself if you are gritting your teeth and trying to handle the situation all by yourself when you might feel better reaching out. Or have you clenched your fists in anger and defiance at your misfortune and, consequently, could not accept a helping hand even if it were offered? If finding a hand up when you bottom out creates a secure and comforting safety net for you, give yourself permission to ask for help when you need it.

I honor what I want and need when I'm in crisis.
I am able to reach out to others for help.
I allow others to give me a hand up.

Acting as the Arms of God

Acting as the arms of God by opening ourselves to service for others is a beautiful pattern we women weave into our safety nets. Lending a hand and an empathetic ear can be a tremendous heart-lift not only for the person in need but also to the person serving. By opening ourselves to the needs of others, we often find that we are "in the flow," where opportunities to be helpful present themselves in the most serendipitous ways.

When we commit ourselves to supporting and comforting ourselves by becoming our own good friends, a natural outcome will be the desire to recycle support by befriending others. The most important door we can open in our desire to be service-full is the one to our own hearts. Loving and accepting ourselves in a genuinely heartfelt way opens our hearts to others and invites God to use us as She sees fit.

I support myself and, in turn, am happy to support others.
I open myself to being service-full.
I welcome opportunities to act as the arms of God.

Risking Business

As women leap deeper and deeper into the often choppy waters of the business world, we face a new breed of fear. Will we succeed or fail? Can we swim with the sharks without becoming one? Do we have what it takes to capitalize on our knowledge, market our wares, and stay afloat in a sea of black, not red, ink?

Many of us are afraid to take the risks that seeing our dreams to fruition would require. One of the best ways to transform our fears is to discover how realistic they are. Some of our fears are based on fact and result from personal experiences; many others, however, are remnants of old inadequacies and beliefs from the past.

Give yourself the gift of facing your fears, gleaning self-awareness from them, and encouraging yourself to risk in spite of them. And remember to turn to friends for support and encouragement. Comforted by the response you receive as well as your own successes, you can more easily trust your abilities and maintain the courage to continue risking.

I face my fears and learn from them.
I encourage myself to live my dreams.
I accept risk as a part of doing business.

Building on Small Successes

Focusing on our successes, no matter how small, is an effective way to pare fear down to a manageable and realistic size. We all have special and significant successes upon which we can build. In order to have a happy and fulfilled life, we need to focus on the "build-ups" rather than the "tear-downs." Yet it's so easy to habitually tear ourselves down by concentrating on our limitations rather than building on our successes.

Building a bridge of small successes can land us on the shore of our aspirations. What small, nonthreatening step can you take right now to help you befriend fear and build your own unique bridge?

I allow myself to take small steps toward my goals.
I accept and trust myself during successful and difficult times alike.

Overcoming Goal Blindness

It is very easy in our rush-rush world to be seduced into a state of goal blindness. We become virtually blind to everything but the specific goal in front of us. When we're afflicted by such blindness, a gorgeous sunset, a friend's birthday, or even our own children's childhood may come and go without our really paying attention. Reachable and realistic goals, interspersed with a few idealistic and hard-to-attain ones, are necessary and healthy; but being blinded by our goals—sacrificing spontaneity, fun, or family life for them—probably means we're being driven by some fear we need to uncover and heal.

Goal blindness leads to rushing, and rushing is dehumanizing and injurious to all living beings, including ourselves. Although it's hard to break the habit of rushing blindly toward our goals, we can do it. With awareness, willingness, and commitment, we can learn to sample in a more leisurely fashion all the delicacies life has to offer.

I give myself permission to bite off only as much as I can comfortably digest.
I take one small step at a time toward rebalancing my life.

Standing by Our Core

The word "courage" comes from a combination of *cor,* which in Latin means "heart," and *corage,* which is French for "the capacity to stand by our core." Standing by our core by having the courage to honor ourselves and value our needs is often difficult if we've been taught to put others first and ourselves second, if at all. It takes a great deal of heart to counter old beliefs about the appropriateness of standing up for ourselves.

Often we feel unsure about living in integrity with our core because we fear moving into a "me, me, me" mode of selfish behavior. The opposite is actually true. The more we honor ourselves by standing by our core beliefs and feelings, the more loving toward others we become.

Having the heart to stand by our core requires that we pare away the layers of "he wants," "they expect," and "I should" in order to find the "I am," "I need," and "I can." By sensitively healing the fears causing us to betray our core, we can become accepting and supportive lovers to ourselves and others.

I have the right to honor who I am, what I need, and what I can do.
I have the heart to love and support myself.

Leaving the Mists of "Someday I'll"

We are surrounded by innumerable opportunities. Possibilities for personal expansion, excitement, and happiness abound. Do we take advantage of them or do we crouch fearfully in the shadows thinking, "Someday I'll learn to speak up for myself, clear up this relationship, write my book…"?

"Someday I'll" does not honor the present, create a positive future or support self-esteem. Hiding in the mists of "Someday I'll" may appear safe, but usually it leaves us filled with regret for things left undone and unsaid.

But what if we're frightened about doing or being something new and have relegated the desired change to "maybe tomorrow"? We need to transform our fear by having the courage to look at it and heal it. We can start by asking ourselves what is keeping us stuck. If you have a dream languishing in the mists of "Someday I'll," gently encourage yourself to examine any fears that may be keeping you from realizing your dream right now. In the warmth of loving self-support, our fears dissipate and we are empowered to confidently follow our heart's lead.

I make decisions easily.
I allow myself to follow my heart's lead.
I do it now.

Blessings of Our Natural Child

Most of us are aware of our wounded inner child. But there is also a natural, playful child inside us. She may be buried deeply under layers of distrust and injury, but she is there and we can recover her. As we become loving parents to ourselves, our natural child will begin to emerge and we'll discover a little person who is curious rather than fearful, spontaneous rather than rigid, helpful instead of resistant, creative instead of bored, and open rather than wary.

If the spontaneous, carefree part of ourselves has gone into hiding, it's probably because we have been overly harsh with ourselves and unintentionally created an emotional climate in which our natural child cannot thrive. The best way to encourage her to appear is to make it safe for her to do so. By treating ourselves gently, we issue an invitation to the little girl that says, "It's safe to be here, Honey! You're welcome to come out and play.

Do yourself the service of recovering your natural inner child. She will bless your life with joy, laughter, and spontaneity.

I am a gentle and loving parent to myself.
I invite my natural inner child into my everyday life.

Reclaiming Childhood Dreams

Were you ever told to stop being silly when you fantasized and imagined as a child? Were your dreams endorsed and encouraged or were they scoffed at by the big people you looked up to? Many of the hopes, desires, and dreams we had as children were indicators of the special gifts we brought into this life. If we have lost track of our dreams, we can reconnect with them now by encouraging ourselves to look back and explore them.

We can reconnect with our dreams and lovingly support ourselves in pursuing them by asking questions such as: What make-believe did I revel in when I was little? Where did I go in my fantasy world? And then, most important, ask: How can I translate my childhood dreams into adult realities?

Our childhood dreams and fantasies are gold mines of possibility. Denying dreams dulls us, but accepting them can energize and motivate us to expand into areas that our hearts have yearned for. Take the opportunity now to reclaim your unique dreams.

I honor and listen to my dreams—current and past.
I give myself permission to play.
I have the right to dream and explore possibilities.

Embracing No-Fault Living

In order to enjoy comfortable and mutually supportive relationships, we need to embrace the art of no-fault living. This doesn't mean that we allow others to walk all over us, but it does mean that we learn to curb our criticism of others and insist they do the same toward us.

No-fault living means accepting and supporting ourselves, our friends, and our loved ones. When there are uncomfortable issues to confront, we discuss them in a way that leads to understanding and solutions but doesn't cast blame.

Everyone is imperfect, and having that fact pointed out to us in a critical fashion (and is there really any other way to do it?) decreases our chances of expanding and enhancing our capabilities. In the face of censure, we become fearful of doing or saying anything and learn to walk on eggshells. Criticism dams the flow of good feelings, whereas encouragement and support strengthen our abilities to become the best we are capable of being.

I always seek the good that is in people and leave the bad to
Him who made mankind and knows how to round off the corners.
—Goethe's mother

Irrigating Arid Situations

Many of us who are concerned about the environment are landscaping our yards with plants and shrubs that are drought resistant and can thrive with very little care and maintenance, creating what is called a xeriscape. This is a responsible thing to do so far as our yards are concerned, but it's not so good for our personal lives. How many of us live arid emotional lives, barely able to maintain our root system, let alone bloom beautifully?

In order to emotionally support ourselves, we need to become gently honest with ourselves about whether or not our lives and relationships are supporting us—giving us enough love and attention to thrive—or whether we're dying of thirst. And we also need to examine whether we are providing enough of the emotional essentials for those we love.

We can learn to water our own landscape and create a flourishing garden out of life. If we're struggling to survive in a xeriscape, we can change that by paying better attention to our wants and needs, and finding and creating springs where we can quench our thirst. From our overflow, we will generously spill out love to others.

From a sense of overflow, I give to myself and others.
I deserve to be cherished and appreciated.

Owning Our Own Projections

One of the best ways to ensure fulfilling relationships is to be confident of who we are and have honest and supportive relationships with ourselves. Why is this so important? Because, to the extent that we don't know ourselves or are blind to our vulnerabilities and prejudices, we will unknowingly project those shortcomings onto those we love.

For instance, if we berate and judge ourselves when we make a mistake, we're likely to think that other people are also judging us when, in fact, they may be completely unaware of the mistake.

We are the authors of our lives, and we can write new, healthy scripts that cast us as lovable and deserving women. As a result, we're more likely to be appreciated by those around us, and our relationships will be enhanced.

I am willing to acknowledge my own projections.
I have the courage to heal emotional wounds
that keep me from having good relationships.
I love and support myself.

Flying toward the Flame

Have you ever felt as though your mind were filled with frantic moths fluttering around the flame of an insult or hurt? Try as we might to tame them, sometimes our thoughts insist on flying in and around the fire of our pain, and we end up feeling scorched by anger or guilt.

If you find yourself moth-minded, try this meditation. Close your eyes and conjure up a picture of your thoughts as moths. Allow yourself to see the flame of your resentment or anger and watch as your thoughts circle dangerously around it. Purposefully fan the flame and encourage it to burn even brighter. Watch as the flame licks and dances. Then very slowly and without judgment begin to deprive it of oxygen by putting something over it to snuff it out. As the flame quietly ceases to burn, gently gather up the moths and release them in a beautiful meadow filled with sweet-smelling flowers.

When we find our thoughts obsessively drawn into the flame of emotional pain, we need to consciously redirect them to a calming image or affirmation that encourages peace of mind.

I can change my thoughts.
I let go of anger and resentment easily.

Calming the Inner Sea

So much of the turmoil in our lives is the result of our need to be right. Often we hold on to a grudge because we righteously know we're right! And maybe we are. But does that stubborn insistence that the other person acknowledge we are right add to our happiness or build a dam between us and him or her?

It's difficult to give up the idea of being right because much of our security and self-esteem comes from believing we are right. But living with the attitude of "They better see it my way" or "I have to be right" leads to a stormy life filled with resentment.

Calming our inner seas by deciding we would rather be happy than right doesn't mean that we acquiesce to others or relinquish our beliefs. It just means that we choose to let go of unimportant things that we have a stubborn tendency to gnaw on, terrier-like.

I calm my inner sea by choosing to be happy.
I allow myself to float free of resentment.
I love and accept myself when I am right and when I am not.

Traveling Tandem and Flying Solo

So many of us have traveled tandem all of our lives. Being intimately linked to others causes us, of necessity, to continually make compromises—conferring on everything from how to budget our money and where to live to what movie to see and what to eat for dinner. And generally we believe that the other person's desires, not ours, come first.

In order to flex our decision-making muscles, it's important to encourage ourselves to fly solo at least a few hours per week. We need time alone to recharge and to renew our ability to know what we want and to do what feels right for us—just us.

Regularly flying solo renews our ability to be truly present to ourselves and, when we accept that it is all right for us to have time alone, we'll also be able to be more loving and receptive to the other people in our lives. Flying solo actually makes us more compatible and compassionate tandem partners.

I make decisions easily.
I am entitled to solitude as well as togetherness.
I know what I want.

Knitting the Raveled Sleeve

Sleep, as Shakespeare said, knits up the raveled sleeve of care. And who among us does not go to bed some nights with substantially raveled sleeves? We need our sleep because it replenishes all of our resources—emotional, physical, mental, and spiritual.

If our sleep vibrations do not mix and match well with our bed partner, this may sometimes mean we need a bedroom of our own. The sleep-on-the-couch cliché does not have to be a derogatory comment on the state of our relationship; rather it can mean that we have supported ourselves by creating a comfortable sanctuary, a feminine haven where we can get our much-needed rest and knit up our raveled sleeve of care, undisturbed.

Sleeping well during the night means we are more likely to have an accepting and supportive attitude toward the people we meet during the day.

I sleep easily and peacefully.
I have the right to sleep in a comfortable, restful place.

Finding Freedom through Honest Feeling

We frequently categorize our feelings as good or bad, acceptable or unacceptable—and attempt to include only the good and acceptable ones in our lives. This usually doesn't work, because feelings are very often illogical and originate from old beliefs and experiences; they are not so easily managed.

Become aware of one feeling you are experiencing right now. With curiosity, not judgment, explore it. If the chosen feeling could take physical form, how might it look? What does it want to say? What does it want to do? How do you feel about it? With good humor and amusement, encourage the feeling to express itself in a positive manner.

By becoming aware of our feelings, accepting them, and expressing them creatively and constructively, we free ourselves to be fully human.

We should not pretend to understand the world only by the intellect;
we apprehend it just as much by feeling.
—*Carl Jung*

Remembering to Breathe

One of the best ways to free our feelings is to breathe into them. Deep breathing assists us in several crucial ways. Physically, it cleanses our bodies of air that has been sapped of life-giving oxygen, replacing it with fresh, rejuvenating air.

Psychologically, slow deliberate breathing allows us to move beyond surface feelings into awareness of root emotions that may be breeding discomfort in our lives. Spiritually, deep breathing connects us to the flow of God's universe, anchors us firmly in our center, and brings us a sense of calm.

But especially when we're tense or in crisis, we literally forget to breathe. This puts us in the position of attempting to cope while being deprived of vital oxygen.

Do yourself a life-enhancing favor. Remember to breathe deeply. Write a little note that says simply, "Breathe," and refer to it several times a day, especially when you need to be sharp and at your best.

The beautiful thing about remembering to breathe deeply is that we can do it anywhere, in any situation. It is guaranteed to improve our lives!

I am thankful for my breath.
In times of crisis I remember to breathe deeply.

Answering "Present!"

Feeling bored or overwhelmed may mean that we are approaching life like an apathetic teenager going to school—not present with enthusiasm but rather existing in a fog of indifference. If we play hooky from life by automatically doing what has to be done and savoring nothing, we're robbing ourselves of the chance to vigorously feel and live life. We are not answering "Present!" when Life calls the roll.

In order to feel vitally alive and live up to our creative potential, we need to make a commitment to being present, up front, and alert in our lives—not slumped in the back row, lethargically waiting for the bell to ring.

Encouraging ourselves to sit in the front row of life helps us to be attentive to and appreciative of all its varied aspects. When we answer, "Present!" we'll be rewarded by conscious living in which we are aware of our feelings rather than separated from them.

I give myself the gift of sitting up front in my life.
I pay attention.
I have a right to really experience my feelings.

Becoming an Inner Environmentalist

We are becoming more responsible for our planet by adopting environmentally conscious ways of living on Mother Earth with the fervent hope that she will thrive and continue to support us. But equally important is an increased awareness of the detrimental consequences of inner pollution, caused by self-condemnation, unsupportive relationships, exhausting schedules, unhealed emotional wounds, and lack of spiritual conviction.

If we are to feel comforted rather than criticized, we must become inner environmentalists, cleaning out unwanted feelings and clearing space for health and wholeness.

No matter where our emotional garbage originated, it is our responsibility now to discard it, heal it, and free ourselves from it. It is possible, with commitment and courage, to become happy, healthy, and emotionally uncluttered.

I have the courage to face and cleanse my inner pollution.
I ask for encouragement and support when I need it.

Removing the Cauldron from the Fire

From time to time, we find ourselves embroiled in a cauldron of discontent, stewing over things we wish were different. When this happens, we can choose to remove the cauldron from the fire by changing our focus to action instead of reaction. For when we allow our cauldron of negative feelings to remain too long in the fire, we become hard-boiled.

Gently center yourself in whatever way works for you, and allow to float into your mind a situation that causes your internal cauldron to boil. What angers you or causes you resentment? Have you allowed yourself to feel victimized by the circumstances? What dash of love toward yourself do you need to add to the equation in order to start changing the situation? Gently assure yourself that you have the right and responsibility to transform these feelings, and commit to supporting yourself in removing your cauldron from the fire.

I have the courage to be assertive.
I listen to my feelings and act on them when appropriate.

Letting the Shadow Roam

According to Carl Jung, the shadow parts of ourselves are undeveloped or denied aspects of our beings that need to be acknowledged. If we were brought up to be "nice" girls, for example, we were probably also taught to be ashamed of our shadow—our rage, assertiveness, ambition, sexuality, even our creativity—ultimately repressing it to the detriment of our well-being.

Denied, our shadow gains strength and becomes almost diabolical in its ability to cause us, and others, pain. But when we embrace our shadowy aspects and learn to express them in constructive ways, their energy is transformed and, and, as a result, is able to merge in a healthy way with our other parts.

Like the dark side of the moon, our shadow is ever present. It is up to us to liberate and illuminate it.

I am a nice person even though I have ugly feelings.
I invite my shadow out to play.

Melting Stress through Motion

Lakes or ponds fed by moving water remain fresh and clear. Similarly, by encouraging ourselves to move, we can transform unwanted emotional stagnation into vitality. Putting ourselves in motion can help us achieve the emotions we would like to have.

Physically, movement facilitates circulation and helps the body process the nutrients it needs; mentally, putting the body into action helps us clear out the cobwebs and makes us sharper. Feeling better physically and keener mentally, in and of itself, makes our emotions more harmonious. We just plain feel better about ourselves when we move.

Encourage yourself to get up and move right now. We still have within us that spontaneous child who intuitively knows how to dance toward balance and harmony. Invite her out to play. Let her remind you of the transformative value of unrehearsed motion.

I enjoy being in motion.
I choose the form of exercise and movement
that is right for me and commit to doing it.
I allow my inner child to dance and play spontaneously.

Accepting What Is

When we can adopt the following simple but profound prayer as our life's creed, we epitomize acceptance in its healthiest form: God, grant me the serenity to accept the things I cannot change, the courage to change the things I can, and the wisdom to know the difference.

Acceptance is a difficult lesson to learn. There are always conditions in our lives over which we have no control, and we can get stuck believing that circumstances should be a certain way, or that people must act in a prescribed fashion. Caught in the intolerance of our "shoulds" and "have to's," acceptance is canceled out. When we clutch resistance tightly to our chests and vow we'll never accept thus and so, we cement ourselves into the situation, attitude, or pain.

The acceptance I am talking about is not giving up or lapsing into hopeless resignation; it is having the wisdom to know when to say, "Ah, this is how it is. How can I have peace of mind in the face of this?"

I find that it is not the circumstances in which we are placed, but the spirit in which we face them that constitutes our comfort.

—Elizabeth King

Viewing Discipline as Desirable

Accepting the fact that we are responsible for our own lives is incredibly empowering. We may have been erroneously taught that we were in charge of making other people's lives happier, but few women have been encouraged to see that, in reality, we are responsible for making our own lives work.

If we are to maintain confidence in ourselves, we must be able to trust that we'll do what we say we're going to do. This requires a healthy amount of self-discipline—not the harsh and strict expectations a critical parent might have, but reasonable and doable self-discipline—such as setting realistic goals and then following through with what we have agreed to do.

Although the word "discipline" sometimes evokes a negative response, it actually comes from the word *disciple,* meaning "a learner who is in loving response to a respected teacher." Viewing ourselves as both a teacher and a learner simultaneously, not as an errant child in need of punishment, helps us do whatever needs doing.

I enjoy being gently self-disciplined.
I accept responsibility for my life.

Accepting Who We Are

To accept who we are and who we are not is a fundamental invitation being issued continually from our higher selves. What a challenge! It is such a temptation to "if only" our accepting ourselves: If only I were more successful . . . If only I were married (or single) . . . If only I were smarter, prettier, wiser . . . then I would be able to accept myself.

Because during our lifetime we are involved in a continual reincarnation of selves—being reborn regularly into new identities, new beliefs, new talents—it is imperative that we learn to accept ourselves now, as we are. We may never get another chance to accept the selves who look back from the mirror today. By tomorrow they may be entirely new peope. If we accept them today, those new women will be happier and more capable than the ones who live in our skin now.

Let us not wait until tomorrow—or eternity—to accept who we are. Let's do it right now.

I deserve acceptance from myself and others.
I am acceptable just as I am.
I accept myself.

Riding in the Change Parade

Life is a constant parade of changes! Some will be inspiring and exciting, making us want to grab our baton, jump in front of the band, and shout for joy. Others will more closely resemble a funeral cortege. In light of its inevitability, befriending change is a comforting philosophy for us to work toward. By looking for the personal growth inherent in any new phase of life, we can make the Change Parade work for us rather than against us.

Doggedly resisting change sets us up to be forever fighting the inescapable, which can eventually lead to feelings of hopelessness and depression. When we master the art of accepting change and commit to making the best of it, we are choosing to evolve—to be vital, useful, and happier people.

I have the courage to accept change.
I allow change to teach me valuable lessons.

Changing What Can Be Changed

Imagine what it would be like if the owner of an aquarium never changed the water in the tank. It wouldn't be long before the fish died, attempting to glean oxygen from a stagnant and used-up source. Changing the water and keeping it circulating allows marine animals to thrive in their habitat. It's much the same with us. Without change, we would stagnate.

Although many of us resist it fiercely, change forces us to grow and evolve, to become more flexible, resilient, and confident. Our task is to transcend any fear of the unknown and encourage ourselves to change what needs to be different in our lives in order for them to flow freely and creatively. A wonderful Zen story tells of a teacher giving a student a silk scarf snarled in many knots. The student's assignment was to free the scarf of the knots, a chore he struggled with until receiving the insight that, in order to succeed, he must untie the knots in reverse order.

Change can be difficult, but by gently untying resistant little knots, our entire scarf can eventually flutter freely in the breeze.

You may be disappointed if you fail, but you are doomed if you don't try.
—Beverly Sills

Facing the Fork in the Road

While standing at a fork in the road, wondering what choice to make, it is important to take into account what is really right for us. So many of us women almost automatically say, "Whatever you want," as we stand on the threshold of a decision, letting others choose for us. Such self-denying, and often unconscious, behavior can cover the spectrum from a simple acquiescence, like not choosing a restaurant, to a major sacrifice, such as giving up a career because someone else disapproves or may be inconvenienced.

Perhaps at a crossroad in our lives we disowned an important dream, ignored the yearning of our hearts, or simply did not do for ourselves what we would automatically have done for a friend. Regrets are born from the resultant feelings of self-betrayal.

We know what is best for us, and when we allow ourselves to really listen to our inner wisdom, we can turn a fork in the road into a genesis of self-respect and self-esteem.

I have the strength to handle the consequences and the rewards of my choices.
I know what is best for me and act accordingly.

Defibrillating Our Funny Bone

If we discover that responsibility and seriousness have shuttled our sense of humor off into cold storage, we can rescue and revive it. We have the power to decide to change our outlook—to lighten it up, to let it bubble rather than grumble.

Sometimes our funny bone, as well as our zest for life, gets buried under fear of ridicule or disillusionment.

Even if we have temporarily forgotten that life can be pretty darned funny a lot of the time, we can choose to remember to take everything less seriously, patch our levity leaks, and let laughter lighten our load.

It might help to find a symbol of playfulness—a picture, a balloon, a clown pin, a puppy or unicorn sticker, whatever—and carry it with you. Glancing at the symbol and consciously reminding yourself that it is okay to play can help resuscitate your levity.

It is up to us to defibrillate our funny bone. Only we have the means to get out our defibrillation paddles, turn on the juice, and then let 'er rip.

I love life.
I have a great sense of humor.
I love to laugh and get excited.

Kicking the Worry Habit

Worry is a habit that knocks the supports out from under us. One of the most freeing changes we can make in our lives is to kick the worry habit. Since most habits are learned, it's important for us to ask where we learned to worry.

The only lasting antidote for chronic worry is faith—in the good, that the Universal Mystery is for us rather than against us. If we have learned to believe in the unfortunate and hateful, we have the ability to change that and come to believe in goodness and love. I know it's possible because I've done it myself, inspired by a little card that I keep in my pocket that reads, "Sometimes we have many reasons to be unhappy and not many reasons to be happy. Our task is to be unreasonably happy."

If you are plagued by the worry habit, simply becoming aware of worry when it overtakes you and deciding to affirm that life is good will set your feet firmly on the road to kicking the worry habit.

What we believe is our choice, and we can support ourselves by choosing to be faith-filled and happy—even unreasonably so.

I am safe.
I believe that life is good.

Keeping Relationships Current

Relationships are as important to us women as the very air we breathe. Without our relationships, we feel bereft, cut off from vital sources of comfort and support. Yet, even with our busy schedules, have we been able to make it a priority to keep our relationships current? Luckily, most of our heart-held relationships, those that add to our lives and multiply our blessings, are fairly drought resistant and can thrive on bursts of concentrated love and attention. But if nurturing and sustaining our relationships feels like yet another energy-draining obligation, we need to change our perception and see friendship as a sacred, life-enhancing gift we give and receive.

Open your heart for a moment and allow your intuition to clue you in to who needs a supportive word from you today. What kindness, compliment, or moment of your time can you give to someone with whom you want to keep your relationship current?

I nurture and sustain my relationships through following my urges to give.
I am a trustworthy friend to myself and others.

Flowing with the Current

Have you ever gone on a river-rafting trip? If you have, imagine what it would have been like if your guide thought it would be interesting to have you go up the river rather than down. The excitement of the trip would wane very quickly as you attempted the arduous task of fighting the current by going against the flow.

We wouldn't accept a guide like that, would we? But in our inner lives, so often we do just that! Daily, our attitudes and beliefs about abundance launch us into the river of life and cause us to struggle upstream.

One excellent way of going with the current is to uproot any self-denying beliefs about money and view prosperity as freedom—freedom to do more for ourselves and to be of better service to others. We need to encourage each other in learning to value our talent by accepting our ability to earn money.

When we believe that we are worthy to receive and that the universe benevolently wishes to give to us, we can flow with the stream of abundance and feel cared for and wealthy no matter what the circumstances.

I deserve to live abundantly.
Life is an abundant blessing, and I am worthy of every smidgen.

Becoming a Conduit of Grace

There are people who seem to be lightning rods for grace. From them flows an almost visible vibration of compassion, and to be around them is to feel blessed and uplifted. Some are saints and some are ordinary people who have the extraordinary ability to allow respect and kindness to flow through them—not all the time, but at least on occasion.

Close your eyes and gently focus on your breathing, allowing it to move in and out naturally. For a few minutes, think of nothing but your breath. Without effort, bring your mind back to your breath as it wanders off. Ask yourself what type of grace you would like to become the conduit for today. Visualize yourself walking through your day as though you already were such a conduit. How does it feel? Notice how your grace-giving affects the people you meet. Allow that grace to flow to you, through you to others, and return to you.

We can become loving conduits for the grace that fits our particular journeys.

I am a conduit of grace.
Love flows to me and through me.

Flying with a Tailwind

Abundance could be described as the knack for living with an attitude of gratitude. If we constantly run on fast forward, frantically trying to keep up with life's demands without taking a break to restore ourselves and count our blessings, we'll soon run out of gas. Stopping for a rest, pausing to really see the wonder in our world, and making room for interludes of thankfulness helps give us the energy to keep going.

Give yourself the priceless gift of extricating yourself from the whirlwind for a few minutes and write down all the things, just within sight, for which you feel grateful. Expand your list to include people and circumstances out of sight. As a bonus, add to your list some intangibles—attitudes, experiences, even philosophies. Look at your list and allow your heart to open in a flow of gratitude and appreciation. Visualize that flow of thankfulness enveloping you like an iridescent mist that embraces all those with whom it comes in contact.

Flying with a tailwind of gratitude helps us savor the effortless times and move more quickly through the turbulent ones.

I am grateful for my life.
I appreciate life, both the chaff and the grain.

Growing through Loss

Loss is unavoidable, and descending into the grief of loss is, initially, a plunge into emotional hell. When racked with raw sorrow, we simply need to survive. In order to heal naturally, and grow through our pain, we must first allow ourselves to feel it.

In spite of the pain, grief can also be the doorway to the rich cavern of our being, the sanctuary of our soul. Growing through loss enables us to evolve into deeper levels of confidence and maturity. When we are committed to growth, we will make the arduous climb out of the pit of loss carrying the precious jewels of strength, resilience, and a greater capacity for empathy and caring.

For those of us who, in our grief, consciously move toward a deeper acceptance and understanding of ourselves and God, the abyss of despair can become an incubator for compassion and spiritual conviction.

I like living. I have sometimes been wildly, despairingly,
acutely miserable, racked with sorrow, but through it all
I still know quite certainly that just to be alive is a grand thing.
—*Agatha Christie*

Cradling a Staggering Heart

Our hearts stagger under the weight of many hurts. Whether the injury is large or small, being cradled by supportive kindness is essential.

Having a tender and accepting attitude toward ourselves while racked with pain provides much-needed inner comfort, but it is imperative that we allow outside support as well. Inner and outer support can combine in miraculous ways.

Close your eyes and place your hands over your heart. For a few quiet moments, concentrate on the rhythm of your heart. Give thanks for its faithfulness. Allow to come into your mind's eye a picture of yourself in pain. With your hands still protecting your heart, compassionately observe the you who is hurting. Who is she? What does she look like? What is she feeling? Who can comfort her? What person or thing outside of her can cradle her as she grieves? Visualize her being comforted in whatever way your wise subconscious presents. Soak in the nurturing, and permit your heart to open and receive compassion and healing.

When in pain, protect your heart as you would a precious infant.

I am as willing to cradle my own heart as I am to cradle others'.

Moving toward Balance and Harmony

Life is an unceasing cycle of birth, death, and rebirth, revolving changes, losses, and gains. Our often difficult lesson is learning to remain balanced and in harmony with ourselves no matter what the circumstances.

In attempting to come to grips with our fluctuating fortunes, we can look to Mother Nature for inspiration. In her is a flowing balance of opposites—warmth and cold, light and darkness, summer and winter. Mother Nature teaches us that there is a season for all happenings. She gives us hope that "this, too, shall pass."

In order to feel more harmonious, do yourself a freeing favor and make a list of ways in which you can support yourself today. Jot down what you want and the areas in which you need to say "no." Maybe more of you needs to be put on the scales of your life in order for them to balance properly.

I accept and incorporate change in my life.
I help balance and harmonize my life by not forgetting myself.
I believe that this, too, shall pass.

Opening the Door to Pain

In order to lovingly support ourselves, we must go gently into the dark nights of our souls—but go in we must. Just as we are taught to turn into the skid on an icy road to regain control of our car, we need to turn *into* our feelings rather than away from them. Only by turning into and then moving through our feelings can we gain control of them and emerge into the light of healing.

Never is it more important for us to take care of ourselves than when we are standing on the threshold of pain. We need to be protected by friends who can listen without judgment and support us unconditionally. But we must also be there for ourselves, cultivating an internal intimacy that is sympathetic, accepting, and trusting.

Opening the door to our pain means that we let ourselves feel it, examine it, and then release it—or at least have an intention to let it go. If we can meet our pain while securely centered in the sacred heart of the Divine, we will be less terrified and more willing to confront it.

I am worthy of resting in the sacred heart of the Divine.
I am a caring friend to myself.
I am supportive of myself and others when a painful door needs opening.

Mourning Invites Morning

Grief is a sleep robber. When you're grieving, those long, black hours from approximately three a.m. to dawn can be the most devastating. Being awake in Mother Nature's darkness forces us to face the darkness within ourselves. Finding constructive ways to mourn in those lonely hours is a tremendous challenge, but we do have the inner strength to accomplish it.

Anger and resistance may be bedfellows that keep us too agitated to sleep. We may want to avoid our emotions because we fear that allowing them would overwhelm us with such rage and sorrow that we would never again regain our equilibrium. If that is the case, it's better to get out of bed and express our feelings through writing them out or drawing a vivid picture, for instance, rather than lying there, becoming more upset and frustrated by the minute.

Grief does feel overwhelming at times, but it's more likely to overpower us when we shun it than it is when we courageously feel it. Avoiding the feelings released so relentlessly during the night only generates suppression, not healing.

I express my grief constructively.
I am strong and able to transcend and heal my wounds.

Wishing at the Well

To love is to risk loss, but not to love is to ensure emotional death. Therefore, if we choose to really live, we will need to accept a certain amount of grief as well. Nobody says, "Oh goody, another opportunity to grow!" when confronted with loss and pain; in fact, our basic wish is to avoid plunging into the well of grief. But sometimes we have no choice. And if we don't avail ourselves of emotional support at those difficult times, we run the risk of closing our hearts in order to escape sorrow.

Within each of us is a wellspring of healing powers. Our task is to be confident that we are equal to our challenges and accept ourselves as powerfully resilient even while feeling frail and vulnerable.

I have a wellspring of healing within me.
I am a survivor.
I can do all things through God who strengthens me.

Re-Potting Ourselves

Loss changes our environment and, therefore, us. It is essential that we adapt to our new conditions by re-potting ourselves, fertilizing and feeding the shaken bloom that we are after a traumatic change, so that our roots can reach into a greater faith and trust in ourselves.

Take a few moments to imagine yourself as a plant or flower. Close your eyes and see or sense the garden or pot in which you are planted. What do you, as a plant, want and need more or less of? How can you provide that for yourself?

We deserve the support and nurturance of our own private spot in the sun. When we are torn from it, we have the strength and wisdom to re-pot ourselves in a way that allows us to heal, while anchoring our roots firmly in new circumstances.

I trust in my ability to heal.
I nurture and protect myself when my roots are exposed.
I turn my face to the sun.

Trusting the Feminine Within

Birth is a miraculous affirmation of our ability to trust the feminine. Don't women, after all, have the awe-inspiring power to accept and incorporate the masculine and, together, create life? I believe that fear of this wondrous power is at the root of our distrust of the feminine. What a responsibility to accept and support such power.

Even if we never give birth to a child, we regularly and naturally conceve, nurture, and birth life in ourselves and others through emotional support and love. Realizing that we carry the power and innate wisdom to generate spiritual, emotional, and physical life, we can have confidence in the feminine within, knowing that she is willing and able to create a balanced and harmonious life for us when we choose to listen to her perceptive counsel.

The Sacred Feminine, in her highest reality, embraces all, synthesizing the divergent and the similar, welcoming both the wounded and the wise to her breast. She honors the Whole and is wholly trustworthy.

To live is so startling it leaves little time for anything else.
—Emily Dickinson

Honoring the Feminine Way

Water, the most powerful and yielding of the elements, symbolizes the feminine way: strong and never deterred from its goal of union with its source, yet adaptable and creative as to the means by which it arrives at its destination. The feminine way is the way of the heart, unfolding and blooming in concert with the natural flow of life.

Visualize yourself as water, strong and powerful yet yielding and adaptable. Explore where you are now and where you want to go as this body of water. Absorb the feminine attributes of the water until you feel as though you have become one with it. Relax in the awareness that, while there may be temporary dams, nothing permanently impedes your journey toward eventual union with your source. If the water you imagine doesn't feel right—too powerful, meandering, frozen, stagnant—change it. Envision exactly what you yearn for from your feminine way. What "water-ness" do you want to bring into your daily life to better express your femininity?

I honor and respect my femininity.
I am able to be strong and flexible.
I trust my ability to flow with life.

Discovering the Sand Dollar's Surprise

When we shake an intact sand dollar, we can hear a little rattle and know that some surprise remains hidden inside. Breaking open the shell reveals five delicate objects resembling doves or angels. If Mother Nature endows the simple sand dollar with angels, can we not trust that she does the same with us?

Although the sand dollar is pretty when whole, it's even more miraculous when broken open. That's a lot like us—although we may look good and function well, we have to break free of old patterns in order to really uncover the marvels within us.

To help you break free, make a list of ways in which you protect yourself. What shells do you hide in? Then write a separate list of the fears that originally made you feel the need for protection. Choose one fear to concentrate on now, and gently close your eyes. Allow a picture of the woman or girl who holds that fear to come into your mind's eye. As much as you can, accept and befriend her. Over time, repeat this meditation with the other fears that have confined you.

We are all laden with gifts and talents that are yearning to be released in order for their blessings to fly free.

I am free to be authentically me.

Reawakening to Wonder

How conscious and awake are we? Do we savor the current moment or squander it in anticipation or dread of tomorrow? One of the reasons children are so good for us is that they remind us to be absolutely present in the here and now. Taking a walk with a small child reeducates us in the ability to give wonder-filled attention to whatever we focus on.

The feminine within resonates to the same miraculous music that children do. It loves beauty and relationships, and savors genuine connections with people, things, and experiences. Reawakening to wonder reconnects us to the childlike attributes of attention and appreciation. Events and feelings become special and sacred when framed in undivided attention. Life becomes a fully conscious experience when made up of moments when we are really real and truly present.

When we realize that life is too precious to sleep through and accept our need to make time for the minutia, we honor the feminine within and support our much-neglected inner child's desire to be awake to wonder. All of life, even the difficulties, can more readily be perceived as miraculous and wonderful when we encourage ourselves to become wonder-full.

I stop and take time to appreciate life's little wonders.

Transforming Archetypal Fears

Many of our fears are grounded in fact. Historians tell us that in the three years of the Spanish Inquisition, nine million women were burned as witches. Later, in our own country, the same fate befell many women in New England. In general, these gender holocausts were perpetrated against women who were sought after for their healing, counseling, and midwifery skills. Their knowledge and wisdom—and in some cases, eccentricity—was perceived as a threat to the "powers that be," and so they were destroyed.

Embedded in our history are two messages: wisdom is punishable by death, and to be fully empowered is to be life-threateningly vulnerable.

What the executioners began with their witch burnings, we have perpetuated through our unexamined personal and archetypal fears. We are changing that, but we still need to transform the ancient fears that continue to lurk in the shadows of our subconscious. Only by bringing these fears into the light, where they can be examined for their present-day validity, will we transform them.

I am safe and protected.
I am wise and empowered.

Finding Solace in the Everlasting Arms

We are in need of comfort regularly, but never so acutely as when we are experiencing pain, loss, or change. It doesn't matter what form they take; as shattering as death or divorce or as simple as a thoughtless remark or moving from one home to another. Whatever the genesis of our feelings or insecurities, the vulnerable part of us yearns for comfort and support that can come from many sources: family, friends, pets, uplifting reading, self-love, and spirituality.

Making a habit of supporting and loving yourself is paramount on your healing journey but, when you have fallen against a jagged place on your path, it is also extremely wise to practice seeking solace from, and trusting your bruised heart to, the Divine Mystery whose arms are forever waiting to guide and console.

The Divine Beloved is in every breath I take.
Underneath are the everlasting arms.

Lighting Our Flame

While meditating on the flame of a candle floating in an iridescent crystal wineglass, I was struck by the similarity of this candle to the potential we all have floating within us. Spiritual promise, our own unique light source, lies waiting to catch fire. We hold the matches, and it's our choice whether we light our interior candle or leave it floating coolly in the shadows.

Our spiritual potential will wait, for it is eternal. But would we not be warmer and happier—more our authentic selves—if we moved through the necessities, joys, and sorrows of our days warmed by the glow of this inner fire?

While contemplating the floating candle, one important thing I noticed was that the imperfections in the crystal showed up more clearly when the candle was burning than they did when it was cold. Maybe the defects amplified by the candlelight are symbolic of the fact that, even when we ignite our flame and consciously travel the path to enlightenment, we will not be perfect. Nor do we need to be. But, by lighting our inner flame, we will cast out darkness.

I am a spiritual being.

Acknowledgments

A huge thank you to everyone at Red Wheel/Weiser for creating such a beautiful little book. An especially heartfelt thank you to Amber Guetebier, whose good humor, professional competence, and unflagging kindness made this project a joy for me.